Promoting Seismic Safety

Guidance for Advocates

FEMA 474 / September 2005

 FEMA

Promoting Seismic Safety

GUIDANCE FOR ADVOCATES

Sponsored by

 FEMA

Developed by

Daniel Alesch

Peter May

Robert Olshansky

William Petak

Kathleen Tierney

Associated with

The Mid-America Earthquake Center

The Multidisciplinary Center for Earthquake Engineering Research

The Pacific Earthquake Engineering Research Center

SEPTEMBER 2005

Preface

This project represents a collaboration among social science and policy researchers at the three Earthquake Engineering Research Centers:

- Mid-America Earthquake Center (MAE)
- Multidisciplinary Center for Earthquake Engineering Research (MCEER)
- Pacific Earthquake Engineering Research Center (PEER)

FEMA asked researchers at the three centers to distill the findings of previous social science and policy research in order to provide guidance to seismic safety advocates. Our hope is that the lessons of prior research will help advocates be more effective at promoting seismic safety actions.

To reach potential advocates, FEMA will provide these materials to partner organizations. Such organizations can then adapt the materials and deliver the content in a relevant format to appropriate members. This is not intended to be a static document for one-time publication and distribution by FEMA.

> **Note:** Sidebars appear throughout this document to explain terms or concepts readers may not have encountered before.

The full version of *Promoting Seismic Safety: Guidance for Advocates* is a 200-plus page report that consists of two parts: Part One is a guidance document for advocates; Part Two is a set of background papers developed by the authors as part of the project. This abridged version of the publication includes the guidance document but not the background papers.

Adobe® Portable Document Format (PDF) files for both the guidance document and background papers can be downloaded from the website of the Multidisciplinary Center for Earthquake Engineering Research at http://mceer.buffalo.edu. To access the PDF files, click on the Publications tab at the top of the page or in the left margin. On the Publications page, click on Online Catalog link in the left margin, which will take you to the Searching and Ordering Publications page. Follow the instructions on this page and a series of links will take you a page that allows downloading the document and background papers in PDF form or ordering a printed copy of the full publication. PDF files for the guidance document are also available on the FEMA website. Go to www.fema.gov and enter "Promoting Seismic Safety" in the search blank.

GUIDANCE DOCUMENT FOR ADVOCATES

This is a collection of concise tips for advocates, organized into the following topics:

- Successful seismic safety advocacy
- Earthquake basics
- The ABCs of seismic building codes
- Policies and legislation
- Appearing before committees
- Informing and persuading
- Partnerships for seismic safety
- Working with experts
- Effective risk communication
- Using the media
- Further reading

BACKGROUND PAPERS

Six papers were developed by the project authors to support and amplify the advice to advocates in the guidance document.

- *Partnership Plan (Peter May).* In order to reach an audience of potential seismic safety advocates, FEMA needs to work with partner organizations to deliver the information in ways appropriate to their members. This paper describes a plan for accomplishing such partnerships.

- *Examples of Successful Seismic Safety Advocacy (Robert Olshansky).* This paper describes—and draws lessons from—advocacy successes in Arkansas, California, Missouri, New York, Oregon, Utah, and Washington. It includes personal stories of the advocates involved in these successful actions.

- *Formulating and Evaluating Policy Alternatives (Daniel Alesch and William Petak).* Drawing on two detailed cases—abatement of unreinforced masonry buildings in Los Angeles and Long Beach, California, and the 1994 amendment to the California Hospital Facilities Seismic Safety Act (SB 1953)—this paper presents a number of lessons on making and implementing policies. It concludes with strategies for devising effective policies and programs.

- *Gaining Attention (Daniel Alesch and William Petak).* Summarizing relevant public policy literature, this paper explores ways to identify appropriate decision-makers relevant to the problem. It provides advice on gaining the attention of persons, organizations, and institutions that can make a difference in reducing the risks to life and property from earthquakes.

- *Communicating Risk (Kathleen Tierney).* This paper provides guidance that will enable advocates to craft effective risk communication messages and campaigns, deal with issues that are unique to earthquake risk communication, and avoid mistakes in communicating clearly about the need for seismic safety.

- *Mobilizing Support (Kathleen Tierney).* Picking up where the previous paper left off, this one gives advocates a better understanding of how to motivate action in support of loss reduction efforts. Presented here are concepts and strategies needed to persuade others to engage in mitigation activities.

The five authors developed the materials through a series of meetings from February 2002 through February 2003. We also acknowledge the active participation of our FEMA project sponsor, Elizabeth Lemersal. Sarah Nathe edited the final version of the guidance document. Finally, we thank the following seismic safety advocates who joined us at some of our meetings and/or provided helpful comments along the way: Mark Benthien, Lind Gee, Marjorie Greene, Bill Holmes, Sarah Nathe, Tom O'Rourke, Chris Poland, Richard Roths, Susan Tubbesing, and Maria Vorel.

Introduction

Promoting seismic safety can be challenging because people seem indifferent to its benefits or decision-makers dismiss good ideas about ways to make buildings and communities more resistant to the damaging effects of earthquakes. Advocates work hard and care deeply, yet often feel that their efforts are ignored. Given these frustrations, advocates sometimes give up, or wait for another day. This resource kit is meant to inspire all advocates to keep working toward their goal. The briefs assembled here distill what we have learned—through research and experience over the last 40 years—about promoting seismic safety in the United States.

We have used a very broad definition of "advocate." Advocates can be almost anyone: people whose jobs involve public safety; design professionals who want to make a difference; those who work in organizations with missions to increase seismic safety; and citizen-activists who have a personal stake in earthquake safety. Many potential advocates do not think of themselves as such because they are not trying to change seismic safety policy. But seismic safety can be increased at levels as various as design and building professional practices, planning commission and special district procedures, and implementation of public safety programs. People who try to increase the adoption and enforcement of seismic building codes or assess the earthquake safety of schools are in fact seismic safety advocates.

Across the United States, advocates have improved seismic safety in areas with moderate to very high degrees of seismic risk by arguing for reduction of future losses in damaging earthquakes, and by calling attention to the economic and social vulnerability of their community to the losses an earthquake could inflict. Especially important to consider are buildings that are built to out-of-date and inferior codes, where people nonetheless live and work.

Successful advocates point out another rationale for seismic safety—more earthquake resilience in highways, power and utility systems, buildings, and communities means increased resilience to other types of damaging events, both natural and human-caused. Talking about seismic issues often has the benefit of raising questions about the condition of facilities or the readiness to respond to any extreme event.

What Is Seismic Safety?

Earthquakes damage structures—buildings, roads and bridges, utility and communications systems—and those damaged structures kill and injure people and cost a great deal to fix. And while the structures are not functioning, the businesses that rely on them either fail or face great financial hardship. Seismic safety advocates attempt to reduce all earthquake losses in various ways. Structures can be strengthened to resist shaking, either when they are built or later in their lives, or they can be sited in areas less subject to violent shaking. But increasing seismic safety requires knowledge of the earthquake hazard in a community or area, an understanding of how to reduce structural damages, and a willingness to spend the money and time necessary to do so. Decisions to invest in seismic safety are made by individuals, private and public sector organizations, and governments, so the goal of seismic safety is served by risk education, community activism, and political activism.

Loma Prieta Earthquake, CA, October 18, 1989 (left to right) – The first story of this three-story apartment building located in the Marina District of San Francisco failed when ground shaking caused liquefaction of the soil on which the structure was built. (D. Perkins, U.S. Geological Survey) *Fifty-one spans of this double-decker freeway collapsed in Oakland, killing 41 motorists.* (E.V. Leyendecker, U.S. Geological Survey) *Northridge Earthquake, CA, January 17, 1994 – A broken gas line on Balboa Boulevard in Los Angeles caused this fire.* (M. Rymer, U.S. Geological Survey)

The Seismic Safety Hit Parade

Seismic safety projects are as various as the communities at risk to earthquake damage, but some projects are common to all areas in the United States because they are critical steps in improving understanding of earthquake risk and inspiring a commitment to loss reduction. You can't undertake all of these at once, and may not need to invest the same level of energy in each one, but sooner or later your journey to increased seismic safety will require you to develop projects in each of the 10 areas below.

1. Improved understanding of earthquakes—learn about quakes from local, regional, state, or Federal earth scientists.

2. Comprehensive analysis of local risk—learn about how quakes damage the built environment from local engineers, emergency managers, academics, state and Federal government experts, and risk analysis firms.

3. Wide familiarity with the many ways to reduce risk—structural engineers, geotechnical engineers, academic researchers, engineering associations, and governmental agencies can explain and recommend the best earthquake-resistant design and construction techniques.

4. Clarified costs and benefits of reducing risk, who pays, and who benefits before the quake and after it.

5. Broad communication of elements in items 1-4, above, to the community.

6. Campaigns to persuade specific audiences that something can and should be done.

7. Wide cooperation among individuals and groups to decide which losses are most important to reduce and how best to do so.

8. Proposal of new practices, procedures, or policies to various groups.

9. Strategies for achieving official adoption by governments and organizations of new policies and procedures that reduce risk.

10. After adoption, it is still necessary to promote, monitor, and enforce actual implementation of policies and procedures because real people in actual situations may not understand why it is important to comply.

The premise underlying the following suggestions is that seismic safety advocates come in many forms and with many levels of knowledge and experience. Each of the following briefs may be more relevant for some advocates than for others. The first three briefs present concepts to know before starting to talk about seismic safety. The second three discuss groups to target in working to improve seismic safety. And the final four briefs describe tools available to seismic safety advocates.

- Successful Seismic Safety Advocacy
- Earthquake Basics
- The ABCs of Seismic Building Codes
- Policies and Legislation
- Appearing Before Committees

- Informing and Persuading
- Partnerships for Seismic Safety
- Working With Experts
- Effective Risk Communication
- Using the Media

Damage to older woodframe houses has been widespread in recent U.S. earthquakes. Newer woodframe houses built to seismic building codes usually do not have such damage.

Successful Seismic Safety Advocacy

Though seismic safety advocates are a diverse group, there is much similarity in the steps they take to succeed in their work. Aspiring advocates can distill a few basic lessons from their tried and true strategies. The most important lesson is that individuals can make a difference. The second is that collectives can leverage the power of individuals. Four additional golden rules complement the first two.

BE PERSISTENT, YET PATIENT

Persistence. It takes time to introduce the importance of seismic safety to the public and to decision-makers. Repeated efforts are necessary to make the case that earthquakes are a threat and that cost-effective actions can be taken to reduce the threat. Those interested in ensuring that their community takes steps *before* an earthquake must convince skeptics that a serious problem exists, that something can be done about it, and that the solution is affordable. All this requires persistence.

Patience. Try to take the long view, and remember that earthquakes are a long-term issue. All successful seismic safety initiatives have had their ups and downs in the process of public debate. Each step, no matter how small, brings you closer to the goal, even if it takes a while to get there. Be incremental.

HAVE A CLEAR MESSAGE

Identify the problem and its solution. In plain language tell your audience what the problem is and how your initiative will solve it. If they do not understand the problem, they will take no interest in the solution.

Propose specific solutions. Propose actions that your audience can endorse and accomplish. Specific solutions are more likely to be adopted and carried out. If the solution is clear, detailed, and specific, decision-makers can readily adopt it when the opportunity arises.

Who Is the Public?

There is no such thing as "the public." There are many publics within a community—individuals, small groups, and large institutions, each with self-identity and self-interest. Depending on the outcome you're working for, various audiences must be educated and persuaded. The media can help you reach many groups and individuals, but at the same time, the media are themselves a group in need of education. At community meetings you will meet other audiences. Just as the public is not one thing, it is not static. The groups and individuals who can support your project will change over time, but a successful advocate will change also to ensure that the seismic safety project and goals remain viable.

Have a message that is clear and consistent. The message must be easily comprehended and remembered. If it is too complicated, your audience will neither remember it nor act on it.

Repeat the message. Find multiple opportunities to present your message to both the narrow and broader audiences you seek to influence—in print, in public presentations, at public meetings, and to the media. Each time you repeat the message, more people will remember it. It is especially effective to present the message after significant earthquakes in your own region or even in other parts of the world because then people are more aware of the actual damages earthquakes can inflict.

UNDERSTAND THE BIG PICTURE

Appreciate the audience's point of view. For most people, earthquakes are not an important concern. Understand your audience's current knowledge and perception of the risk. Explain the importance of seismic safety in a way that is meaningful to them. Remember that citizens and elected officials must be convinced that reasonable steps can be taken to protect against the earthquake threat at reasonable cost or they will not act.

Identify a good audience for your effort. Rather than trying to reach all the people all the time, focus your energy on a small set of people inside or outside of government who can understand the earthquake risk and commit themselves to action. They will then influence larger groups to reduce future losses.

Link seismic safety to other issues. Point out how seismic safety also addresses other community issues, such as the safety of schoolchildren, protection against other hazards, fiscal health of the local government, and long-term sustainability of the local economy. In particular, show how seismic safety can preserve businesses and public sector organizations, and thereby stabilize the tax base or ensure the continuity of government and educational institutions. Those are important day-to-day public issues. Similarly, proposals for enhanced earthquake safety will be more acceptable if they are part of a multi-hazard protection package. It is possible to design and implement precautions that protect against many perils: high winds, storms and storm surges, willful acts of destruction, and industrial accidents.

Identify potential opponents. Various groups will come forward with arguments against seismic safety actions. Identify these opponents early on, meet with them, and try to understand their perspective. At least be familiar with their arguments. Chances for success will increase if you can involve them, develop consensus solutions, and gain their support.

The media are your friends, but use them wisely. The media have the power to communicate your message widely. They can also gain the attention of decision-makers. Before approaching the media, be sure that you have a clear message as well as broad support from local seismic safety professionals.

WORK WITH OTHERS

Create partnerships and build coalitions. Identify potential allies and partners who can gain from promoting seismic safety. The support of other organizations and individuals can be the critical difference between success and failure. Start with your own networks, and then reach out to other relevant professionals and community organizations. Be sure that partners gain appropriate recognition and praise.

Personal contacts are vital. Develop friendly, trusting relationships among the people you must work with, including your allies, potential opponents, and decision-makers. Make yourself known as reasonable, credible, and responsible. Know whom to call, and when to call them. Organizations are important, but they consist of individuals who make decisions about whether or not to take action.

Make seismic safety efforts permanent. Try to develop organizations, procedures, statutes, or regulations that institutionalize seismic safety. These can range from state seismic safety advisory committees, to city building code commissions or professional organizations. Seismic safety advisory committees are particularly valuable, because they can extend your efforts, maintain public awareness of seismic safety, increase credibility of the message, develop and promote solutions, and build on previous successes. Formal groups frequently bring with them some financial resources, and even modest funding for a new organization or process can provide powerful leverage.

Earthquake Basics

There are characteristics of earthquakes and their risks that you must be clear about yourself before you start talking about them to others. Over the years, earth scientists, engineers, and others who spend much of their time studying earthquakes have developed a set of terms relating to earthquakes that have very precise meanings, but that are often confusing or meaningless to those outside the field. This brief highlights some of the key concepts that commonly arise in discussions about seismic safety.

EVERY EARTHQUAKE IS UNIQUE

Each earthquake is a unique combination of characteristics: location, magnitude, depth, type of fault, mechanism of fault rupture, and direction of rupture. In addition, the soils in the area determine how fast seismic waves move, how quickly their energy dissipates, and whether or not they focus on particular sites. Thus, although we like to draw lessons by comparing one earthquake to another, these comparisons can only go so far.

MAGNITUDE IS THE USUAL MEASURE OF AN EARTHQUAKE

The magnitude of an earthquake describes the absolute size of the event. It is a measure of the energy released by the earthquake. Generally, higher magnitude earthquakes have greater shaking intensities at the epicenter, shake for a longer time, and affect a larger area. Several magnitude scales are currently in use, and they are all different, especially for larger earthquakes. The well-known Richter scale is one magnitude scale, but seismologists have increasingly begun to favor the *moment magnitude scale* because it gives more reliable results for larger earthquakes and those more distant from recording devices.

INTENSITY IS ANOTHER WAY TO DESCRIBE AN EARTHQUAKE'S SIZE

Earthquake intensity scales qualitatively describe the effects of ground shaking rather than the energy released. While an earthquake is described by a single magnitude, it will produce a range of shaking intensities across an area. Because the intensities describe what the shaking feels like and how it affects different types of structures, they are terms that most people understand. In the United States, we use a scale that ranges from Intensity I ("Not felt except by a very few under especially favorable conditions") to Intensity XII ("Damage total"). Intensity is usually greatest near the earthquake epicenter, and less away from the epicenter, but it can increase in certain areas of poor soil.

EARTHQUAKES OF SIMILAR MAGNITUDES MAY HAVE DIFFERENT EFFECTS

Two earthquakes of magnitude 6.5 can cause dramatically different levels of ground shaking because they may differ in depth or mechanism of fault rupture. The 2001 magnitude 6.8 Nisqually earthquake, for example, shook a wide area near Seattle but caused much less damage than the 1994 magnitude 6.7 Northridge earthquake in Los

Angeles because the Nisqually earthquake was extremely deep and did not cause severe shaking at the earth's surface. Earthquakes of similar magnitude can also cause differing levels of damage according to their proximity to populated areas. The 1995 magnitude 6.9 earthquake in Kobe, Japan, was much more devastating than the Northridge quake because the strongest shaking was in the most densely populated areas of Kobe, whereas the strongest shaking in the Northridge quake was under the mountains north of Los Angeles.

Northridge Earthquake, CA, January 17, 1994 – Buildings and personal property were all destroyed when the earthquake struck.

Kobe Earthquake, Japan, January 17, 1995 – A relatively tall, reinforced-concrete shear wall building completely tipped over into the street. The roof of this building cut through the building across the street. (Copyright 1997 by Earthquake Engineering Research Institute)

SMALLER EARTHQUAKES CAN CAUSE DAMAGE AND INJURIES

Earthquake damage at any given point depends on magnitude, distance to the rupture, the local soil conditions, and the building types, so even smaller magnitude earthquakes (between 5 and 6) can cause considerable damage and injuries in particular localities.

SOFTER SOILS ARE USUALLY LESS SAFE THAN FIRM GROUND

Generally speaking, softer soils shake more than firmer soils. Sandy and water-saturated soils can also experience *liquefaction,* in which the ground turns to mush during the shaking and loses its ability to support structures.

IT'S NOT ONLY ABOUT THE FAULT LINE

Everyone in a seismically active region should be concerned, not just those located "on the fault line." Because earthquake waves radiate out from faults and cause damages over large areas, seismic safety precautions are important region-wide. It is more important to worry about overall seismicity of an area than to know only the location of faults. The most current U.S. Geological Survey seismic hazard maps of the United States are at http://earthquake.usgs.gov/hazmaps.

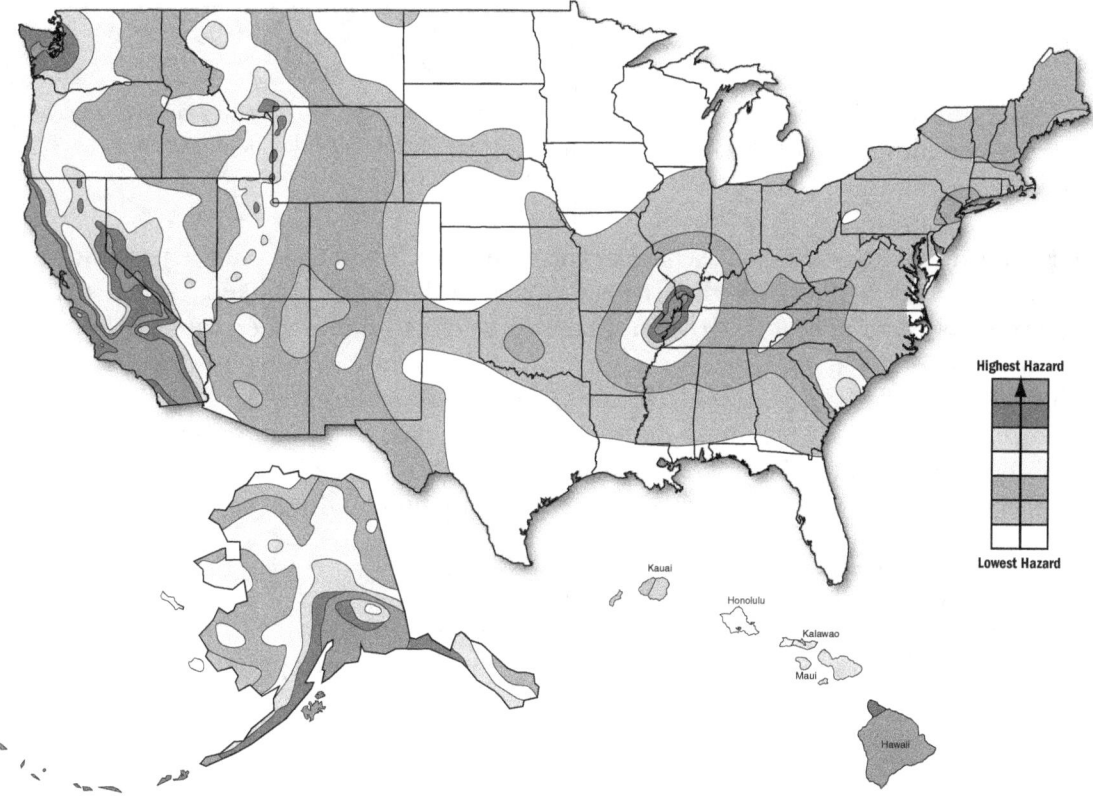

Earthquake hazards in the United States. This map is based on seismicity and fault-slip rates and takes into account the frequency of occurrence of earthquakes of various magnitudes. Locally, the hazard may be greater than that shown, because site geology may amplify ground motions. Based on U.S. Geological Survey National Seismic Hazard Map for the Coterminous United States (http://eqhazmaps.usgs.gov/html/map_graphic.html).

Source: U.S. Geological Survey.

UNKNOWN FAULTS OFTEN CAUSE EARTHQUAKES

Earthquakes can strike on faults that were previously unrecognized. Many such earthquakes, for example the 1994 Northridge quake, have been extremely damaging. Because, by definition, earthquakes on unknown faults can't be anticipated, it is more prudent to focus on an area's overall seismicity in determining its earthquake risks.

SEISMOLOGISTS CAN ESTIMATE LONG-TERM EARTHQUAKE PROBABILITIES

Based on historic earthquakes and evidence of prehistoric earthquakes, seismologists are able to estimate the long-term probabilities of earthquakes in seismically active areas. These estimates, however, are only approximate, because we do not have enough years of records to make statistically reliable estimates. The estimates are useful as a basis for seismic building codes, as well as for comparing hazards between regions, and do give some indication of the likelihood of future damaging earthquakes.

Aerial view of the San Andreas fault in an undeveloped area of the Central Valley in California.
(Source: NOAA National Geophysical Data Center)

We know where large earthquakes have occurred in the United States in the past few hundred years. We know that similarly large earthquakes will occur again, and in some places more probably than in others. We do not know precisely where or when they will happen or how strong they will be. When speaking with a lay audience, it is generally better to avoid technical terms like "expected return period," and to say something like, "From historical evidence, we expect an earthquake on this fault about every 180 years, and it has been 179 years since the last one." Earth scientists also say, "An earthquake of this magnitude in this area has about a 50-percent chance of happening sometime in the next 30 years."

SHORT-TERM EARTHQUAKE PREDICTION IS NOT POSSIBLE

Seismologists are not able to predict imminent earthquakes, as a weather forecaster can predict a hurricane. Due to the physical characteristics of fault rupture, such predictions may never be possible. Because earthquakes occur without warning, increased seismic safety is vital.

An Earthquake Can Occur at Any Time

If seismologists say that a damaging earthquake has a 50-percent chance of occurring in your region during the next 30 years, that can be translated to mean that it has approximately a 2-percent chance of occurring in any given year. The probability is the same this year as it will be next year or 2 years from now. People often speak of earthquakes occurring sometime in the future, but the truth is that they can happen *right now*. Because earthquakes occur without warning, communities must be prepared in advance. There are many options for a community. They can take steps to reduce the number of unsafe old buildings or move people out of them. They can adopt codes that ensure new buildings will be earthquake-resistant. They can strengthen vulnerable buildings. They can modernize their infrastructure and make it more damage-resistant. Or they can reduce the financial consequences of damages through insurance.

Northridge Earthquake, CA, January 17, 1994 — Many roads, including bridges and elevated highways, were damaged by the 6.7 magnitude earthquake.

What Is Infrastructure?

A community is served by many networks, utilities, transportation routes and systems, and communications systems that support the daily flow of life and commerce. These infrastructure elements are frequently damaged in earthquakes and, when they are, can threaten lives and property, and seriously disrupt the routines of community life. Fires can result from downed electrical wires or ruptured gas mains. Interruptions to water, sewer, electrical power, or gas service will affect the lives of everyone, very negatively over time. Interruptions to communications will quickly have large personal and business impacts. Broken transportation links make it difficult or impossible for life or commerce to flow anywhere. Damage to one or two infrastructure elements poses a problem that most communities can work around, but damage to all or most of the elements is a disaster that will cause everything to grind to a halt. Protecting infrastructure against earthquake damage is very important and can be accomplished either through retrofit or replacement.

Northridge Earthquake, CA, January 17, 1994 — Broken gas and water mains on Balboa Boulevard in Granada Hills created this scene of fire and flood. The fire burned five homes. (Copyright 1997 by Earthquake Engineering Research Institute)

Kobe Earthquake, Japan, January 17, 1995 – A bus filled with holiday skiers stopped just short of disaster on a damaged section of the Hanshin expressway. (Copyright 1997 by Earthquake Engineering Research Institute)

The ABCs of Seismic Building Codes

Seismic building codes are one of the most obvious ways to increase building integrity and ensure the future safety of communities. Codes are not a panacea for all problems, so it's helpful to know how they work and what they can do. Incorporating new or additional seismic safety provisions in codes for new buildings has been easier than designing, enacting, and implementing requirements for retrofitting existing buildings, but even if all new buildings are built well, older buildings remain hazardous. Where huge stocks of old buildings are very vulnerable to earthquakes, as in the East and Midwest, net improvements in seismic safety will be marginal if seismic elements in codes apply only to new buildings.

WHAT SEISMIC BUILDING CODES CAN DO

Seismic building codes result in earthquake-*resistant* buildings, but not earthquake-*proof* buildings. Seismic codes are intended to protect people inside buildings by preventing collapse and allowing for safe evacuation. Structures built according to code should resist minor earthquakes undamaged, resist moderate earthquakes without significant structural damage, and resist severe earthquakes without collapse. Codes only recently began to address mitigation of nonstructural, or content, hazards in buildings, which can cause casualties and expensive damage.

BUILDING COLLAPSE IS NOT THE ONLY PROBLEM

Even if a building does not collapse in an earthquake, it can still seriously hurt or kill people. Buildings are full of nonstructural components such as light fixtures, heating ducts, windows, and suspended ceilings that can fall on people or block escape routes. Finally, plaster, falling bricks, parapets, window glass, or the facades of buildings can seriously injure people walking by or exiting.

EVEN CODE-COMPLIANT BUILDINGS CAN BE DAMAGED

The contents and interiors of code-compliant buildings may be extensively damaged in an earthquake and the building may not be functional until repairs and clean-up are completed. Therefore, damages to code-compliant buildings can be costly. Comprehensive safety and loss reduction programs include properly designing and bracing nonstructural elements.

NEWER BUILDINGS ARE GENERALLY SAFER THAN OLDER BUILDINGS

Because they are built under more advanced codes, newer buildings are usually (but not always) safer than older buildings. Steel-frame high-rises and newer woodframe low-rises are usually (but not always) the safest structure types. Exceptions to those generalizations

Model Building Codes

When a municipality decides to adopt or revise a building code, it generally chooses a model construction code and amends it in various ways into its codes and ordinances. In 1994, the International Code Council (ICC) was established to develop a single set of comprehensive and coordinated national model construction codes, among which is the International Building Code (IBC). The founders of the ICC are the Building Officials and Code Administrators International, Inc. (BOCA), the International Conference of Building Officials (ICBO), and the Southern Building Code Congress International, Inc. (SBCCI). These three organizations previously administered three different codes: the National Building Code (NBC), the Standard Building Code (SBC), and the Uniform Building Code (UBC). The presence of three model building codes had the disadvantage of allowing widely divergent code standards across the country. Recently, the National Fire Protection Association (NFPA) developed a national model code, the NFPA 5000. States and localities that currently write their own codes or amend the model codes have begun adopting the International Codes and the NFPA 5000. Both the IBC and NFPA 5000 contain up-to-date seismic provisions; adoption and enforcement of either of these codes will lead to higher quality construction and consistent code enforcement in earthquake-prone areas.

are due to variables such as the configuration of the building, the quality of the construction, the design of the joints, and the manner in which seismic waves strike a particular site.

OLDER BUILDINGS ARE FREQUENTLY NOT SEISMICALLY SAFE

Generally speaking, seismic codes did not come into wide use in the eastern United States until the early or mid 1990s. In the western United States, seismic codes made substantial improvements in construction as early as the mid 1970s. Buildings constructed prior to these respective dates in each area are probably not seismically safe. Retrofitting buildings to achieve seismic resistance is possible, but often costly, so choices must be made about which buildings are most important to fix. It makes economic sense to target the most dangerous structures or the most dangerous features of those structures, such as flimsy parapets.

SEISMIC CODES VARY ACROSS THE UNITED STATES

The seismic provisions of building codes are based on earthquake hazard maps that show the probabilities of certain levels of earthquake shaking in particular areas. The code requirements reflect the fact that some places are more likely than others to have strong earthquakes. The entire country is not required to meet the same seismic design standards as the state with the greatest risk: California. Places that have less severe and less frequent earthquakes have less stringent design requirements. For example, seismic codes require less in Boston than in Los Angeles. Conversely, seismic code requirements in southern Illinois, near the New Madrid seismic zone, are much stricter than in Chicago, which is less likely to have a strong earthquake.

ADHERENCE TO SEISMIC CODES IS NOT AS EXPENSIVE AS MANY THINK

Complying with a seismic code adds relatively little to the costs of a structure. The most recent study estimates that it adds less than 1 percent to the purchase price of a home, and from 1-2 percent to the total cost of new commercial and industrial buildings. (See *Promoting the Adoption and Enforcement of Building Codes,* in the **Further Reading** section.)

SOME STRUCTURES ARE MORE IMPORTANT THAN OTHERS

Buildings with high occupancy, critical response services (fire, police, hospitals), and vulnerable populations (schools, nursing homes) should be built to code, or above it. It is also important to protect utilities and infrastructure. Damages to critical structures lead to more life loss, larger economic loss, and greater social disruption, and they slow community response to earthquakes.

BUILDING CODE ADOPTION IS A STATE OR LOCAL RESPONSIBILITY

All states have a legal right to regulate building safety as a matter of public welfare. In most states, the day-to-day aspects of this rest with local governments. Some states require local adoption and enforcement of building codes; others do not. Just because codes are required, it does not guarantee that all localities comply. And in states that do not require codes, localities are free to do as they wish. In fact, many earthquake-prone communities in the United States do not have up-to-date building codes with seismic provisions.

CODES CHANGE OVER TIME

The model building codes and the seismic provisions are revised every 3 years to incorporate new knowledge. In order to have a code that reflects the current state of the art in seismic design, state and local governments need to incorporate the latest seismic details into their codes.

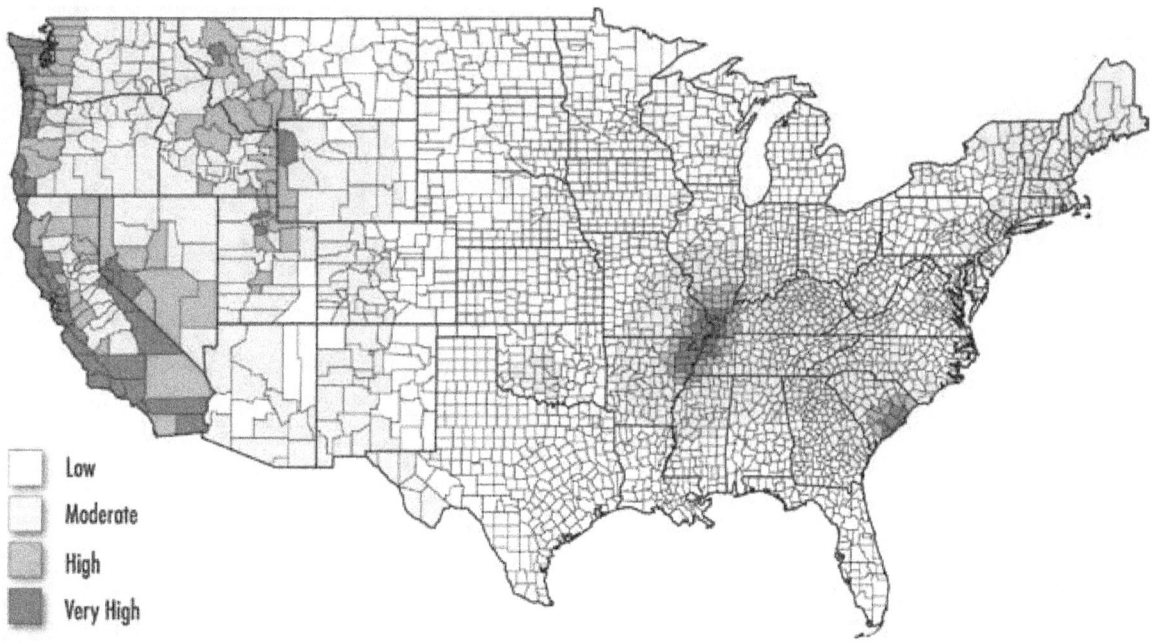

Low

Moderate

High

Very High

Counties in the United States and their probabilities of earthquakes of varying magnitude. Source: U.S. Geological Survey.

BUILDING CODES VERSUS SEISMIC PROVISIONS

Localities can adopt a model building code, but leave out the seismic requirements; or they may have an older version of the code, written prior to inclusion of seismic provisions. It is important to verify that the locally adopted code contains the most recent seismic provisions.

A BUILDING CODE MUST BE ENFORCED IN ORDER TO BE EFFECTIVE

Building plan review, construction inspection, and a qualified and trained building department staff are necessary for code enforcement.

Policies and Legislation

In many cases, it will be most effective to make the primary case for earthquake safety to a few key decision-makers in the public sector. Policy-making processes are complex, but not hopelessly so, and policy-makers are accessible, if you "know where they live." New policies and laws are proposed and enacted almost every day. Once enacted, policies must be implemented, and that is often more complicated than policy adoption. With foreknowledge of the ins and outs, however, you will have a much better chance of success.

LEARN HOW "THINGS WORK" IN THE LEGISLATIVE OR EXECUTIVE AGENCY

High school civics classes teach that policy processes follow an ordered procession, involving, for example, 13 steps for a bill to become a law. In reality, public policy-making is anything but linear and predictable. Although they share many rules and procedures in common, each legislative and executive policy-making body has unique characteristics. Typically, you can learn what the formal rules are directly from agency personnel, but it is more difficult to learn informal processes and hidden agendas. If your own elected representative shares an interest in seismic safety, he or she may be of great help.

HAVE PUBLIC POLICY PROPOSALS READY WHEN THE TIME IS RIPE

Usually elected officials create policies to solve problems after a crisis has occurred. For example, a policy decision to raise the level of a causeway or a levee usually comes shortly *after* the flood. Most earthquake-related legislation is enacted in the immediate aftermath of a damaging earthquake – in what is called the "window of opportunity" – but not all of it is well conceived. The old adage is that we "legislate in haste and repent at leisure." Advocates seeking to influence policy should be prepared with proposals that are thought through and ready for consideration and adoption during the rush of concern that follows a damaging earthquake.

GAIN ACCESS TO POLICY-MAKERS WHO WILL CHAMPION SEISMIC SAFETY

Policy agendas are crowded and it is difficult to gain the attention of policy-makers. The effective earthquake safety advocate must get access to policy-makers and their staff to make the case for seismic safety policies. Access is easiest in the immediate aftermath of a damaging earthquake, especially if advocates have coherent and effective proposals in hand. This is because concern for earthquake safety is on everyone's mind then, demanding attention to possible solutions from policy-makers.

Being a member of public or quasi-public organizations charged with helping to develop seismic and building safety policies provides continual, institutionalized access to policy-makers. Several states have boards or commissions charged with making recommendations about seismic safety. Similarly, non-governmental groups draft building code updates for consideration and adoption by governments.

GET A CRITICAL MASS OF POLICY-MAKERS TO AGREE ABOUT THE PROBLEM

A problem is not a problem unless a critical mass of policy-makers sees it and agrees that something can be done about it. Advocates may view the potential for major losses from earthquakes as a problem that demands immediate attention by public policy-makers, but not everyone will agree. Policy-makers must concur that there are potential unacceptable consequences from an earthquake within a relevant timeframe, and that they are willing to do something to reduce the consequences.

National Seismic Safety Policy

The National Earthquake Hazards Reduction Program (NEHRP) was established in 1977, under the authority of the Earthquake Hazards Reduction Act of 1977, enacted as Public Law 101-614. The purpose of NEHRP is to reduce the risks to life and property from future earthquakes. The NEHRP research and mitigation activities are funded by four primary Federal partners— FEMA, the National Institute of Standards and Technology, the National Science Foundation, and the U.S. Geological Survey. NEHRP funds basic and applied research into earth science, building and infrastructure performance and design, and information dissemination by governmental and non-profit agencies working on many aspects of earthquakes and seismic safety. These Advocacy Briefs were developed with funds from NEHRP.

Learn more about NEHRP at http://www.fema.gov/hazards/ earthquakes/eqmit.shtm.

POLICY-MAKING IS LARGELY POLITICAL AND ECONOMIC, NOT TECHNICAL

Enhancing seismic safety policy requires political and economic understanding as well as geologic and engineering knowledge. Having solutions that meet political, social, and economic criteria is as important as having solutions that are technically effective. Have on hand not only examples of what can be done, but also evidence of how those steps have been effective in other places, and information about how much each solution costs. You must convince the already overburdened that doing something provides benefits at costs that are generally tolerable.

PROPOSE WORKABLE SOLUTIONS

A workable solution must have an acceptable price tag, sufficient backing to overcome opposition from credible opponents, and evidence of having worked somewhere else. Legislators rarely invent solutions – they get them from experts, other advocates, and other jurisdictions that have addressed the issue. The savvy policy advocate works to gain support from others who have an interest in the problem or who might be affected by implementation of the proposed solution. Most elected officials do not like to have proponents and opponents of a particular policy proposal besieging them; they are happy when all the involved parties come to them with a policy proposal in hand and generally agree that it is the best way to move ahead.

NOT ALL POLICIES ARE REGULATORY

Policies may be designed to focus attention, as is the case with the official establishment of April as Earthquake Awareness Month in California or May as Tornado Awareness Month in Wisconsin. Policies may also force action, either directly or indirectly. For example, California has an Earthquake Hazards Mapping Program that directs the Geological Survey to map earthquake hazards all over California, and requires public and private parties to use the maps in assessing the potential hazards to any proposed development. If the risk is high in a certain location, the developers must incorporate appropriate mitigation into the project or they must relocate. Policies may call for public investment, provide for more effective system management, or authorize direct action by public agencies to reduce earthquake risks; for example, increased seismic safety in federally owned buildings was mandated by Presidential Executive Order 12941 in 1994.

Self-policing policies are more cost-effective than those that require extensive monitoring and control. Such policies provide strong incentives for individuals and organizations to engage in the desired behavior either by lowering the costs (monetary and non-monetary) of doing what is hoped for, or by raising the costs of engaging in undesired behaviors. The former case is exemplified by a number of city programs in California that waive many fees normally associated with residential construction and shorten the permit process in order to encourage homeowners to strengthen their houses against earthquakes. Obvious instances of the latter case are the state governments that heavily tax tobacco products and use the generated funds to conduct public education campaigns about the dangers of smoking.

POLICY ENACTMENT IS JUST THE BEGINNING

Policies adopted by legislative or executive bodies are formal statements that put forth what the policy-makers want the general rule to be. Policy is modified through the layers and sets of actors that deal with it, right down to the person in the field who does the work directed by the policy. As implementation proceeds, it may trigger new or additional opposition to the policy, with threats of modification or repeal.

To stand the test of time, policies must strike a balance among various parties interested in the problem being addressed. Frequently, policies that were devised and supported by seismic safety advocates are subsequently challenged by groups whose interests are adversely affected by those policies. In the case of ordinances requiring seismic strengthening of old buildings, the challenges are often effective, at least until the next earthquake. Advocates can be successful in getting what is needed if they are prudent and thoughtful about what they propose, particularly if they keep a few points in mind.

DESIGN POLICY TO MEET THE LEGITIMATE NEEDS OF LIKELY OPPONENTS

The community of seismic safety proponents is small and, in most locations, without much political clout. There are usually many interests likely to oppose the costs associated with enhanced seismic safety. Look at the problem in the broad context to identify legitimate interests that will be positively and negatively affected by any proposal. The greater the burden perceived by the opposition, the more fiercely they will fight the advocate's proposal.

Devise solutions to the problem that meet the fundamental, legitimate needs of those who would otherwise be opposed. This requires willingness to compromise and a creative, non-dogmatic approach to policy design. A policy enacted into law is more likely to remain in place over the long term if it is supported broadly by those it affects than if it was enacted over the opposition of groups with an important stake in the outcome.

REMEMBER THAT NOTHING LASTS FOREVER

A policy that was effective and appropriate at one time may become ineffective and inappropriate as conditions and circumstances change. Problems "morph" out from under solutions. The challenge for those interested in seismic safety is to adjust strategies and policies as circumstances change. The challenge is made more difficult by the nature of legislation; only rarely can it be written to provide sufficient flexibility to deal with both a wide range of initial circumstances and underlying shifts in the context.

Appearing Before Committees

At some point in his or her career, a seismic safety advocate may be invited to appear before legislative or advisory committees that have roles in shaping seismic safety policies. These bodies may include school boards, municipal councils, state legislatures, Congressional committees, advisory committees like city and county planning commissions, or code committees. The suggestions below will help make the experience comfortable and productive.

DO YOUR HOMEWORK ABOUT THE COMMITTEE AND THE PURPOSE OF THE MEETING

Before scheduling meetings with committee staff or agreeing to testify, establish the relevance of the committee to the issues that you want to address. Be clear about the purpose of the hearing you will be attending and your testimony's fit with that purpose. It makes little sense to appear before a committee that is neither the correct forum for the topic nor concerned with the specific issues you are going to raise.

BE CLEAR ABOUT WHAT YOU ARE ADVOCATING

In crafting suggestions to the committee, be clear about your facts, the problem, and the solutions you wish to advocate. Focus on two or three key points to get across. A sea of facts about a problem or heart-wrenching stories about harms do little to help a committee understand what you want them to do to address the problem.

PREPARE A SIMPLE AND DIRECT MESSAGE

Committee members are not likely to be experts on seismic safety so your testimony should educate committee members in an informative manner. Detailed or technical points can be submitted in written testimony for the record or as background materials for interested staff and committee members. Usually, only a short time is available for testimony, so fill it only with critical information.

ESTABLISH YOUR CREDENTIALS

Introduction to written and oral testimony should clearly establish who you are and, most importantly, whom you represent. Establish the type of expertise you have and the breadth and depth of the group that you represent. The logic for this is that elected officials, in particular, respond to groups rather than to individuals. It is important to mention that the group you represent endorses your comments.

CONVEY CREDIBILITY THROUGH DELIVERY

Present your information in a convincing manner. Use charts that display relevant information (as handouts or displays). List sources for your information. Acknowledge counter claims and point out why they are not accurate. Maintaining eye contact with committee members is an important way of subtly establishing credibility.

ANTICIPATE THE ENVIRONMENT FOR THE HEARING

Many who testify are tripped up by not having the proper equipment available, not realizing that the committee is running behind (or ahead), not being able to adjust testimony to a shortened timeframe, being thrown off by other testimony, and not being prepared for any media that might be present. Anticipate potential hiccups by checking ahead on arrangements, knowing who else is involved and the format for the session, being prepared for all media personnel, and being ready to adjust the length of your testimony.

PRACTICE YOUR REMARKS AND RESPONSES TO QUESTIONS

Practice to gain comfort with the material you are presenting. A rehearsal will allow you to assess how clearly you can communicate with your audience. It helps if the practice sessions are in front of some individuals familiar with the perspectives of the actual committee audience. An important part of such practice sessions is anticipating questions that may come up.

BE PREPARED FOR QUESTIONS

Not all questions can be anticipated, but many can and should be. Like the testimony itself, responses to questions should be succinct, accurate, and credible. Resist the temptation to guess if you do not know the answer. It is better to respond that you will find out the answer and respond later in writing. Saying "I don't know" is acceptable as long as it is not the only response you can offer to each question.

FOLLOW UP

As committee procedures allow, edit your comments for the record to correct any mistakes in your own or others' testimony. Promptly send in written responses to questions you could not answer at the time. The written record of any testimony is often more important than the testimony itself. It has a longer shelf life and reaches many more people.

WORK WITH STAFF

Committee staff members are more than gatekeepers; they are also information conduits and repositories of knowledge for committees. It is as important as the testimony itself to help them by making written materials available in advance, providing timely follow-up to questions, and responding to their concerns. A good relationship with the staff can result in repeated invitations to appear before committees.

Informing and Persuading

Some people think that the only way to improve seismic safety is to get a policy enacted or changed at the local, state, or Federal level, but there are actually many other effective ways to do it, most of which are easier or quicker than new policies or amended legislation. There are various interventions that can improve seismic safety.

PROVIDE INFORMATION ABOUT THE EARTHQUAKE RISK

No individuals or organizations will take action to reduce risk unless they know it exists, they think it may affect them, and they know they can do something about it. Before proceeding to any of the steps outlined below, develop messages for key decision-makers and those who influence them. Tailor all information to each audience's sophistication. To make the messages believable, have them delivered by people who are specialists and/or are thought of as credible by the target audience.

Presentations of earthquake risk information can be made more effective through the use of maps and other visual aids designed to address the specific needs and interests of individual decision-makers.

INFLUENCE GOVERNMENT AGENCY PRACTICES AND PROCEDURES WITHIN EXISTING POLICIES

It is not necessary to change laws to influence what government does. Even without new laws, governments can choose to increase the seismic safety of the facilities within their purview and improve community services. Local public utilities rarely need to change ordinances to design and build more resistant structures. Community building departments can encourage and enforce seismic safety practices. Training can affect field practice within the letter and spirit of existing ordinances to focus more attention on seismic safety provisions. Building and planning departments, emergency management offices, and housing agencies can provide seismic safety information to their constituencies. Governments can choose to rent only facilities that incorporate seismic safety design elements. School boards can choose to reduce the nonstructural hazards in their classrooms. Universities can add natural hazards risk management to business and public administration curricula.

INFLUENCE CHOICES MADE BY PRIVATE ORGANIZATIONS

Ultimately, seismic safety is enhanced when structures are located, designed, and constructed appropriately. Sometimes, it makes sense to work directly with individuals and organizations that build and use the structures, rather than to try to change the legal or regulatory environment. Seismic safety can sometimes be sold to individual organizations if it is incorporated at tolerable costs when structures are being built or changed to realize other, unrelated benefits, such as increased organizational efficiency or more structural compatibility with new processes.

Direct communication by shareholders, managers, employees, or third parties may induce a corporation's leaders to promote seismic safety in their own operations and structures. Rate payers can influence utilities to better protect water, gas, electric power, and wastewater systems against earthquakes. Organizations already committed to seismic safety can influence other businesses and not-for-profit organizations. Trade and business associations, such as Chambers of Commerce, can be reached through groups focused on earthquake risk reduction, such as the Building and Industry Council on Emergency Preparedness Planning in the Los Angeles area, or through organizations dedicated to bringing an earthquake safety message to the community.

INFLUENCE PROFESSIONALS WHO CAN MAKE A DIFFERENCE

In states where there are frequent earthquakes, many design professionals have adjusted their practices to reflect the risk. In areas where earthquakes occur only rarely, design professionals may focus more of their attention on snow and wind loads. National and international professional associations can influence their member engineers, architects, and builders to pay more attention to seismic safety issues. Regulators like building inspectors can direct more attention to seismic safety considerations. Those who participate in code development organizations can be reached by official spokespersons. Urban land use planners can take seismic hazards and risks into account when creating community plans or participating in decisions about transportation or housing projects, or other development initiatives.

Risk management professionals for public and private organizations can consider seismic safety in the decisions they make. Traditionally, risk managers have not focused much of their attention on reducing threats posed by natural hazard events, but professional practice appears to be changing. There is increased attention to reducing organizational losses from earthquakes, as well as from other natural events and willful acts. Insurers and market intermediaries, for example, financiers, can play critical roles in improving seismic safety. If insurers and lenders provided improved rates for buildings that are built to withstand greater seismic forces, owners would have greater incentive to design and build their structures that way.

Professional certification and licensing education and training programs can be modified to include appropriate material, whether offered through universities or professional associations. Professional associations can emphasize seismic safety practices in their regular conferences and workshops. Standards for peer review can incorporate attention to seismic safety.

Partnerships for Seismic Safety

Do not try to "go it alone." Successful seismic safety advocacy garners the support of other constituencies within the community. Emphasize the benefits from enacting seismic safety measures while building coalitions and networks capable of sustaining interest and action.

UNDERSTAND HOW DIFFERENT STAKEHOLDERS VIEW SEISMIC SAFETY

Some stakeholders are active proponents of earthquake safety, but others are indifferent or actively oppose enhanced safety measures. Understand what motivates both supporters and opponents. Devise strategies for keeping supporters on board over the long run, neutralizing opposition to earthquake safety, and motivating those who are indifferent. Be willing to compromise and engage in political tradeoffs. Rather than holding out for ideal programs that have little chance of gaining support, gauge which seismic safety options have the best chance of being adopted and implemented under different circumstances.

PROVIDE INCENTIVES

Carrots and sticks make things happen. Incentives can include direct economic rewards, relief from regulation, subsidies of various kinds, low-interest loans, technical assistance, tax breaks, transfers of development rights, and public recognition and awards for those who support seismic safety. Worries about legal liability may also be a powerful motivating force for some stakeholders. Stress how measures taken to enhance earthquake safety help reduce other risks or provide secondary benefits. Champions and partners are important for moving policies and programs forward, but they also like to receive rewards and recognition for their support.

LINK SEISMIC SAFETY TO ISSUES PEOPLE ALREADY CARE ABOUT

Earthquake safety shouldn't be only about earthquakes. Link it to other issues such as homeland security, economic sustainability, environmental protection, quality of life, livability, school safety, and historic preservation. Many of these issues already have organized constituencies that can be "co-opted" into supporting earthquake loss reduction. Sell earthquake safety to these groups by showing how seismic loss reduction yields benefits such as more open space, a charming historic downtown, or better preparedness for terrorism and bioterrorism.

BUILD NETWORKS THAT CAN LAST

Strategies for enhancing earthquake safety must go beyond one-time educational campaigns and single ballot efforts to create long-term networks of seismic safety supporters. Build on existing networks—consisting both of the "already converted" and of groups that can be persuaded to put seismic safety on their agendas. Many groups have already identified themselves as advocates. Other potential candidates for membership in earthquake safety coalitions include structural engineers' associations; groups representing the design professions; building and safety officials; citizens' emergency preparedness groups; neighborhood watch groups; coalitions focused on neighborhood safety, improvement, and quality-of-life issues; victim advocacy groups formed in the aftermath of other disasters; community colleges; and colleges and universities.

GET EXPERTS IN YOUR GROUP

Get to know university-based experts in the earth sciences, the social sciences, and engineering, as well as your local emergency management agency, other key governmental agencies, and important non-profit organizations like the American Red Cross. These ongoing partnerships will help bolster your case for enhancing seismic safety and lend credibility to your efforts.

Moderated workshops and presentations can be an effective means of involving, informing, motivating, and maintaining the interest of stakeholders with varying positions on seismic safety measures.

USE OTHER COMMUNITIES AS EXAMPLES

Learn about and publicize what other communities are doing to address earthquake risks, and use their success stories to obtain support for the measures you are advocating. Get to know the champions in those communities; they can teach you about what to do and what not to do. Frequently, a mayor, city manager, or council member from a community that has adopted seismic safety measures can influence counterparts in a community that has yet to commit to seismic safety. Arrange talks or lunches during which the already converted officials can share their experiences.

Working With Experts

Every seismic safety advocate needs to draw upon experts from other fields. Some citizen activists may need lots of expert assistance. The advice below will help you find and use experts.

DRAW ON A VARIETY OF FIELDS

One expert alone cannot possibly address all concerns regarding seismic safety. Useful experts may include geologists, seismologists, geotechnical engineers, structural engineers, lifeline engineers, urban planners, building officials, economists, lawyers, and emergency managers. Learn the differences in these fields of expertise in order to best match the expert to the issue at hand.

FIND CREDIBLE EXPERTS THROUGH CREDIBLE SOURCES

Because it might be hard to tell who is an "expert," you will need to do some investigating. To seek an appropriate expert, begin with credible sources: state geological surveys, local universities, or professional associations and their local or state chapters. Use experts who are respected in their profession and have proven to be credible to other audiences.

QUESTION YOUR EXPERTS

Do not hesitate to ask for explanations and clarifications from the experts you work with. If you cannot understand their points, neither will most audiences.

USE ENTHUSIASTIC EXPERTS THAT CAN PERSUADE OTHERS

Because you need the support of key professional groups, it is helpful to find experts who have the enthusiasm to mobilize the support of those groups. A network of experts can advance your issue more successfully than just one expert.

DON'T BE SURPRISED WHEN EXPERTS DISAGREE

Experts often have opposing viewpoints on particular issues. What if another expert disagrees with your expert? If the experts you rely upon have good reputations and draw support from their professional networks, your chances improve of weathering controversy and convincing decision-makers, the media, and the public. Acknowledge differences and then arrange a meeting among experts. A compromise position may be possible. The other experts may have valuable points, and incorporating them in your argument will only improve it.

AN OPPOSING EXPERT CAN UNDERMINE YOUR CASE

Experience shows that just one opposing expert, no matter how discredited his or her claims, can undermine a technically well-founded position. It is important to anticipate opposing arguments, and to vigorously and persistently stay with your course of action. However, stick to the facts and do not ridicule an opposing expert, as that will reflect badly on you or your expert's credibility.

OPPOSING NON-EXPERTS CAN BE TROUBLE, TOO

When confronted with the claims of unqualified "experts," you need to marshal your professional experts to counter the claims quickly, clearly, and comprehensively. Develop a convincing explanation and repeat it. Many self-proclaimed "experts" are not experts at all. Expertise in one discipline does not carry over to other subjects. Misrepresentation of expertise is particularly common in earthquake prediction.

DISAGREEMENT AMONG YOUR EXPERTS LOOKS BAD

Your own experts may have points of disagreement, given the complexities of the disciplines relevant to seismic safety. But airing those disagreements in public can undermine your case. Prior to making public statements, your experts should identify points of agreement upon which to base your position, and be willing to acknowledge points of disagreement, if necessary.

It may be helpful to arrange formal meetings with your experts to ensure that their knowledge, communications skills, and enthusiasm are adequate to help you obtain the support of key professional groups. Also, opposing views among experts can be discussed and evaluated so that disagreements can be resolved or at least clearly explained.

REPORTS WRITTEN BY EXPERTS CAN HELP SUPPORT YOUR CASE

Although it is very helpful to have experts who will advocate publicly, you may not find willing participants at first. In the absence of living, breathing experts, cite credible reports. These come from government agencies, reputable consultants, or university professors. Reports on websites are easy to find, and sometimes useful, but Internet information is not necessarily reliable. Experts unwilling to become spokespersons may still give advice on the most appropriate and credible documents.

Effective Risk Communication

With the exception of some residents of California and a few other western states, most Americans have never been in a damaging earthquake, don't expect to, and see little or no reason to protect themselves against one. Even in areas where there has been extensive experience with earthquakes, seismic safety messages must be continually reinforced. As with any risk, people must be regularly encouraged to improve their safety. Well-crafted communications campaigns can help seismic safety advocates achieve those goals.

BEFORE GOING PUBLIC, DEVELOP AN OVERALL STRATEGY

When communicating with the public, policy-makers, decision-makers, or any other audience about earthquake hazards, it isn't enough to focus only on the scientific information you want to convey. It is important to think about the following:

- the audience or audiences you want to reach,

- the distinctive characteristics and needs of those audiences,

- how to be seen as credible and trustworthy by those audiences,

- the best form for communicating scientific information on the earthquake threat (how the content of risk messages should be organized), and

- which media (print, electronic, face-to-face communication) and vehicles (news conferences, brochures, mass mailings, public meetings) will be most effective in reaching target audiences.

KNOW YOUR AUDIENCES

"The public" is very diverse, consisting of many different groups with different informational needs and retention capacities. A one-size-fits-all approach to communicating with them is almost sure to fail. Legislators, policy-makers, private-sector decision-makers, and the general public differ in their information requirements. Be prepared to express the same general point—that there is a significant earthquake risk—in many different ways for your various audiences. Consider what each audience needs to know to make good decisions about the earthquake threat. This will be based both on what you think they require and what they themselves may have expressed.

BE CREDIBLE

People will not act on information given to them by individuals and organizations they do not believe or trust, so analyze who would be the best spokespersons to communicate with different groups. Sometimes these spokespersons are well-respected earthquake experts, and they have gained the respect by adapting their message and delivery to various audiences. Do not assume that all experts can communicate clearly; many have trouble "speaking the language" of non-scientific audiences. When you do not have access to earthquake experts who can communicate well, find people or organizations that are credible to your audiences and ask them to serve as spokespersons for your earthquake-related messages.

The credibility of organizations and individuals can be harmed if they:

- take positions that appear to audiences to be unjustified, based on what those audiences already know,

- make statements that contradict what was said previously or that are inconsistent with information the audiences obtained from other sources,

- communicate about the earthquake threat in ways that appear to be self-serving, or

- gain a reputation for deceit, misrepresentation, or lack of full disclosure.

Once lost, credibility is difficult to regain.

ORGANIZE YOUR INFORMATION TO BE UNDERSTANDABLE AND MEMORABLE

Scientists are comfortable handling complex technical information, appreciating the implications of probabilistic statements, and retaining large amounts of data, but many other people are not familiar with such concepts. To make complicated ideas relevant, understandable, and interesting to non-experts, simple statements and good visuals are essential. Printed materials and brochures are appropriate for non-experts because they can be referred to as needed. In campaigns that rely heavily on radio and television, simple statements and repetition are especially important.

TELL PEOPLE WHAT TO DO

Once you have people's attention about the earthquake risk, it is very important to explain to them what they can do to reduce the possible damages. Include in your messages not only information on concrete steps they can take to protect themselves, but also where they can go for more information – both on the earthquake risk and on the various loss-reduction measures you are recommending.

USE MULTIPLE MEDIA

Effective communications campaigns use mass media and person-to-person contact. They employ all types of media and a variety of information "vehicles" (press conferences, radio and television public service announcements, newspaper and TV feature stories, public meetings). Generally, people process information slowly. They base decisions on what they learn from the media after they have discussed it with their families, co-workers, and neighbors. Reinforce media messages through more personalized ways of delivering information, such as neighborhood meetings and school and workplace preparedness programs.

Communication Tools

Various computer-based resources can be used to improve risk communication. By graphically demonstrating the potential losses from an earthquake in a local area, they can help people "see" the problems they may need to cope with. Geographic Information Systems (GIS) are convenient places to store basic data about the local environment—natural as well as built—and the local or regional infrastructure. Loss Estimation Models go a step further and allow for those data to be manipulated to show probable damages from earthquakes of specific location and magnitude. HAZUS-MH is such a loss estimation tool developed by the Federal Emergency Management Agency. Using GIS technology, the HAZUS-MH software allows users to project earthquake damages and losses to many structures: highways and bridges, schools, hospitals, and residences, as well as to estimate resultant deaths and injuries and potential medical care and shelter needs. Local groups can enrich the basic HAZUS-MH data with locally specific data, thereby making the tool more precise in its projections. For more information on how to acquire and use HAZUS-MH, visit FEMA's website: www.fema.gov/hazus.

BE CONSISTENT

Always keep messages consistent across different media and vehicles, and among diverse groups. Risk communicators have learned that, when people get contradictory pieces of information about what to do, they do nothing. They do not pick a favorite and get on with it. Consistency will require that you work closely and carefully with all your partners—individuals and organizations—but it is worth your while to do so.

Using the Media

Good relations with the media are essential for effective seismic safety advocacy. The public looks to the media as significant sources of information on earthquakes, earthquake preparedness, and earthquake policy. Media sources—newspapers, radio, TV, Internet— have the ability to influence public opinion and to place seismic safety on the policy agenda. This brief offers suggestions to those responsible for developing media strategies, as well as to those who may become spokespersons with the media.

Advice for Media Strategists

BEFORE CONTACTING ANY MASS MEDIA SOURCE, DEVELOP A COMMUNICATIONS PLAN

Establish a timeframe reasonable for different media initiatives, taking into consideration both the time needed to develop media messages and important dates, such as earthquake anniversaries. Divide the labor, assigning responsibility for writing, speaking, arranging media contacts, and other tasks associated with a campaign. Select one or more

Be prepared to take advantage of opportunities afforded by the media, especially in post-event situations, to present earthquake hazard information and promote seismic safety programs and risk reduction activities that will lessen the affects of future earthquakes.

spokespersons who will communicate directly with the media, making sure that they are both credible and comfortable interacting with the media. Your plan should cover approaches and messages during routine times before a disaster and the messages and strategies you may use after an actual earthquake event in your area or nearby. In advance, think about what you want to communicate, and when you want to do so.

MEDIA SOURCES MAY FIND YOU BEFORE YOU FIND THEM

If media representatives contact you before you are ready, say something. At the very least, thank them for their interest. Don't make things up. Don't let them pressure you because they have a deadline. If they ask you a question you can't answer, say you will check facts and get back to them. Do your homework quickly and then get back to them. Or recommend an expert who can answer their questions. Never say anything that would damage your cause or hurt your allies if it showed up in print.

THE MEDIA ARE DIZZYINGLY DIVERSE

There are more media outlets now than ever before, appealing to very diverse audiences. New media such as cable television and the Internet coexist with more traditional print and electronic media. Media usage is highly segmented, with different age, ethnic, and other social groups getting specialized information from various media sources. This variety makes launching public media campaigns extremely challenging, and potentially very expensive.

MEDIA HAVE DIFFERENT STRENGTHS AND WEAKNESSES

Mass media differ in terms of what kinds of and how much information can be conveyed, the impression the information is likely to make on audiences, and how easy it is for audiences to access and refer back to that information. They also differ in terms of "market share," in that some media (network television) reach a larger proportion of the public than others on a typical day. Additionally, media outlets differ in terms of the costs associated with delivering information. In crafting media campaigns, think through these differences carefully.

UNDERSTAND THE NEEDS OF DIFFERENT MASS MEDIA OUTLETS

Establish long-term relationships with people who work in media organizations so that they will assist you in your work. View the media as collaborators in your advocacy efforts and work with media representatives in ways that make their jobs easier. Give the media representatives what they need and they will cover what you want them to. Many media work on very tight deadlines. Be flexible enough to handle the very short timeframes associated with breaking news, as well as the longer timeframes permitted by in-depth and feature stories. Television requires good visuals—always have some or be able to suggest great images. Local television news typically consists of short spots with short messages. More substance can be communicated in print than through electronic media.

Advice for Spokespersons

DEVELOP SKILLS THAT ENABLE YOU TO WORK WELL WITH THE MEDIA

- Don't use scientific jargon. Learn to talk in plain and simple language.

- Don't be afraid to say that you don't know something, and don't feel pressured to respond immediately to difficult and complex questions that require more thought. If more information is needed in order to address a question, say so, and then get that information.

- Keep your message consistent, and remember what your audience needs to know.

- Don't let anyone divert you from conveying your message.

ADOPT A STYLE THAT ENABLES YOU TO RELATE TO YOUR AUDIENCES

- Be honest, but also speak and carry yourself in a way that conveys trustworthiness.

- Be genuinely responsive to concerns that are raised, even when those concerns seem outlandish or unfounded.

- Never treat the media or members of the public dismissively or convey the impression that you think their questions are trivial or silly.

- Allow yourself to act easygoing and approachable. Avoid appearing arrogant to audiences.

- Recognize and address the emotional dimensions of issues that are being discussed, especially in situations that involve controversy.

Advice for Both

MANUALS AND COURSES CAN HELP YOU DEAL WITH THE MEDIA

Developing good relationships with the media is hard work, but there is information available to help with a range of communications challenges, from speaking with reporters after an earthquake to formulating effective letters to the editor and opinion pieces for newspapers. You don't have to wing it. FEMA has training courses for media relations, as may your state office of emergency services. Local non-profits may be another source of training, along with university extensions and professional trainers. There are books, too.

Further Reading

About Earthquakes

Earthquakes, Fourth Edition, by Bruce A. Bolt. W.H. Freeman and Company, 1999:
http://www.whfreeman.com/bolt

U.S. Geological Survey Earthquake Hazards Program website:
http://earthquakes.usgs.gov

U.S. Geological Survey National Seismic Hazards Mapping Project website:
http://geohazards.cr.usgs.gov/eq/

About Earthquake Loss Reduction

Association of Bay Area Governments Earthquake Preparedness website:
http://quake.abag.ca.gov

Earthquake Engineering Research Institute website:
http://www.eeri.org

Federal Emergency Management Agency website:
http://www.fema.gov/hazards/earthquakes

Federal Emergency Management Agency, *Developing the Mitigation Plan: Identifying Mitigation Actions and Implementing Strategies*, How-To Guide #3:
http://www.fema.gov/fima/planning_howto3.shtm

About Buildings and Other Structures in Earthquakes

Mid-America Earthquake Center website:
http://mae.ce.uiuc.edu/

Multidisciplinary Center for Earthquake Engineering Research website:
http://mceer.buffalo.edu

Pacific Earthquake Engineering Research Center and National Information Service for Earthquake Engineering website:
http://nisee.berkeley.edu

About Building Codes

International Code Council website:
http://www.iccsafe.org

National Fire Protection Association, **NFPA 5000**:
http://www.nfpa.org/index.asp

Promoting the Adoption and Enforcement of Building Codes, by Robert B. Olshansky. Federal Emergency Management Agency, FEMA 313, 1998. Available from FEMA Publications: 1-800-480-2520.

Seismic Considerations for Communities at Risk, Revised Edition. Building Seismic Safety Council, FEMA 83. Available from FEMA Publications: 1-800-480-2520.
http://www.fema.gov/hazards/earthquakes/nehrp/fema-83.shtm

Federal Emergency Management Agency, **Understanding Your Risks: Identifying Hazards and Estimating Losses**:
http://www.fema.gov/fima/howto2.shtm

About Seismic Safety Policy

California Earthquakes: Science, Risk, and the Politics of Hazard Mitigation, by Carl-Henry Geschwind. Johns Hopkins University Press, 2001

California Seismic Safety Commission website:
http://www.seismic.ca.gov

Natural Hazard Mitigation: Recasting Disaster Policy and Planning, by David R. Godschalk and others. Island Press, 1999.

Western States Seismic Policy Council website:
http://www.wsspc.org

About Public Education

Disaster Research Center, University of Delaware website:
http://www.udel.edu/DRC

University of Colorado Natural Hazards Center website:
http://www.colorado.edu/hazards

"Public Education for Earthquake Hazards," by Sarah Nathe and others. **Natural Hazards Informer**, November 1999:
http://www.colorado.edu/hazards/informer/infrmr2/infrm2wb.htm